YOU CHOOSE
BOOKS™

W9-AXZ-051

WORLD WAR II
ON THE HOME FRONT

An Interactive History Adventure

---

by Martin Gitlin

Consultant:
Timothy Solie
Adjunct Professor
Department of History
Minnesota State University, Mankato

CAPSTONE PRESS
a capstone imprint

You Choose Books are published by Capstone Press,
1710 Roe Crest Drive, North Mankato, Minnesota 56003.
www.capstonepub.com

Books published by Capstone Press are manufactured with paper
containing at least 10 percent post-consumer waste.

Library of Congress Cataloging-in-Publication Data
Gitlin, Marty.
  World War II on the home front : an interactive history adventure /
written by Martin Gitlin.
      p. cm.—(You choose: history)
  Includes bibliographical references and index.
  ISBN 978-1-4296-6019-8 (library binding)
  ISBN 978-1-4296-7998-5 (paperback)
  1. United States—History—1933–1945—Juvenile literature.
  2. World War, 1939–1945—United States—Juvenile literature.
  3. United States—Social conditions—1933–1945—Juvenile literature.
  I. Title. II. Title: World War Two on the home front.
  E806.G57 2012
  973.91—dc23   2011033542

Editorial Credits
Catherine Neitge, managing editor; Bobbie Nuytten, designer; Wanda Winch, media researcher;
      Laura Manthe, production specialist

Photo Credits
Corbis, 14, 72, Corbis: Bettmann, 12, 89, 97, Hulton-Deutsch Collection, 51; Franklin D.
Roosevelt Library: cover, 30, 39, 83, 102; Library of Congress: Prints and Photographs Division,
23, 48, 64, 67, 75, 99, 101; Maxwell Air Force Base, Alabama, 87; National Archives and
Records Administration (NARA), 6, 9, 10, 19, 21, 27, 33, 35, 59, 68, 92, 104, NARA: CPhoM.
H.S. Fawcett (Navy), 46; National WASP WWII Museum, Sweetwater, Texas, 43

Printed in the United States of America in North Mankato, Minnesota.
022012   006609

TABLE OF CONTENTS

ABOUT YOUR ADVENTURE

YOU are living in the United States in the early 1940s. The world is at war. How will you help your country fight for its freedom?

In this book you'll explore how the choices people made meant the difference between life and death. The events you'll experience happened to real people.

Chapter One sets the scene. Then you choose which path to read. Follow the directions at the bottom of each page. The choices you make will change your outcome. After you finish one path, go back and read the others for new perspectives and more adventures.

YOU CHOOSE the path
you take through history.

Adolf Hitler, the leader of Germany and the Nazi Party, stirred up hatred of Jews.

THE COMING OF WAR

The guns fell silent in 1918. World War I was over. Many called it "the war to end all wars" because they believed such a terrible conflict could never happen again. But they were wrong. Only 21 years later, war would again engulf the world.

Dictator Adolf Hitler and the Nazi political party took control of Germany in the early 1930s. The country had fallen into a deep economic depression. Hitler targeted the Jewish people, whom he blamed for Germany's economic problems. He also blamed German misery on the 1919 Treaty of Versailles that had followed the fighting. It had punished Germany for starting World War I. It also forced Germany's government to pay billions of dollars to its European neighbors.

7

Turn the page.

Meanwhile, storm clouds gathered over Asia. Japan had invaded China. Many Americans were alarmed by the events in Europe and Asia. But they had big problems at home. The Great Depression that began in 1929 left about 25 percent of Americans unemployed. Millions were poor, and many were homeless. Americans were too concerned about finding their next meal to worry about a potential war thousands of miles away.

That potential war in Europe became a terrible reality when Germany invaded Poland on September 1, 1939. Soon Great Britain and France declared war on Germany. But few could have imagined how powerful a military the Germans had developed. Germany quickly conquered Poland and several other countries. The world was shocked when the Germans took over France in just six weeks.

A woman couldn't hide her misery as she dutifully saluted the invading German Nazis.

Some Americans believed the United States should enter the war. But many Americans were isolationists who felt that their country should stay out.

Turn the page.

Everything changed December 7, 1941. That morning hundreds of Japanese planes attacked and destroyed a U.S. naval base at Pearl Harbor in Hawaii. More than 2,000 Americans were killed.

The United States entered World War II after the 1941 attack on Pearl Harbor.

Congress quickly declared war on Japan. A few days later the United States was at war with Germany as well.

The battle lines had been drawn. Germany, Italy, and Japan had formed an alliance called the Axis. The United States joined the Soviet Union, Britain, and other nations to form what was known as the Allies.

Men and women from all over the United States signed up immediately to join the war effort. Millions of men were drafted to fight and sent overseas. But the war didn't just affect the new soldiers. It changed the lives of all Americans.

To be a woman married to an American soldier fighting overseas, turn to page 13.

To be a 12-year-old boy in San Diego, turn to page 47.

To be a wounded black war veteran from the segregated South, turn to page 73.

DAILY NEWS
Copr. 1941 by News Syndicate Co. Inc. **NEW YORK'S** PICTURE NEWSPAPER Trade Mark Reg. U. S. Pat. Off.

FINA

average net paid circulation for November exceeded
aily --- 1,925,000
nday - 3,750,000

l. 23. No. 142 New York, Monday, December 8, 1941★ 64 Main + 4 Manhattan Pages 2 Cents IN CITY LIMITS

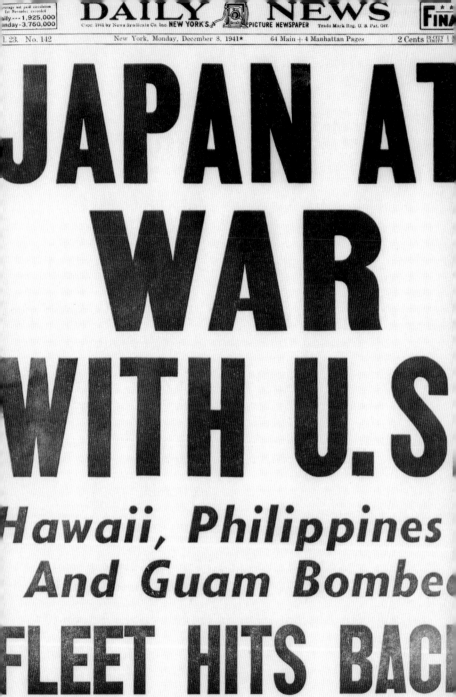

JAPAN AT
WAR
WITH U.S.
Hawaii, Philippines
And Guam Bombe
FLEET HITS BAC

Stories on pages 2 a

CHAPTER 2

TO WORK OR NOT TO WORK

It's a relaxing afternoon in December 1941. You're with your husband, Edward, and a few of your friends in your New York City apartment. Soft music is playing on the radio, but nobody is paying attention to it.

Suddenly, everyone is quiet. A news report has interrupted the music.

"We have witnessed this morning the attack of Pearl Harbor and a severe bombing of Pearl Harbor by army planes, undoubtedly Japanese," states the announcer. "It's no joke. It's a real war."

Turn the page.

President Roosevelt spoke to Congress the day after the attack.

You've never even heard of Pearl Harbor, but you know this indeed means war. The party is over.

The next day you listen to President Franklin D. Roosevelt on your radio. He calls December 7 "a date which will live in infamy." The United States is at war with Japan.

You stare at Edward. He says nothing, but you know what he's thinking. You know he's going to join the fight. You just don't know when.

The following day you find out. Edward packs his bags and enlists in the Navy. You don't know if you will ever see your beloved husband again. Will your 9-year-old daughter, Elizabeth, grow up without a father?

You are feeling lonely and afraid. Should you stay in New York and find a job? Or should you join your wealthy mother in Virginia? You can stay at her home without having to work. But you also want to do your part for the war effort.

➤ To find a job, turn to page **16**.
➤ To move to Virginia, turn to page **18**.

You're like most married women of the time. You have grown used to cooking, cleaning, and taking care of your family. Edward made a fine living in advertising. But now his large income is gone. You need money to pay for food and rent.

One day your friend Edna tells you that a local steel plant has been converted to a factory. It produces fighter planes and other aircraft. They're looking for female workers to replace the men who have become soldiers.

"When are you going over there?" you ask.

"Right now," she answers. "Do you want to come?" The need is so great that you are hired after a 10-minute interview. Soon you are operating heavy equipment that makes sheet metal for planes.

After an eight-hour day on the job, your muscles are aching and you are exhausted. But you are proud of your work.

You realize that you are capable of being more than a mother and housewife. You are just as productive on the job as the men. But then you discover something. The men make more money than the women!

You tell Edna that you're going to complain to the boss, but she warns you to keep quiet. You realize it probably won't help to gripe, but you feel it's a matter of right and wrong. On the other hand, you don't want to lose your job.

➤ To keep quiet even though you're mad, turn to page **19**.

➤ To complain to the boss, turn to page **29**.

The first few months in Virginia are ideal. But you begin to question your decision to stay at home with Elizabeth and your mother. You ask yourself, "What are you doing to help the war effort?" Your answer? "Nothing."

You think back to the flying lessons you took in college. You also recall reading an article in the newspaper about women flying planes from factories to military bases. Other women are testing rebuilt planes. You consider becoming a test pilot.

You can also do more right here in Virginia. You could volunteer to help the soldiers and the war effort.

�%➤ To stay in Virginia and do volunteer work, turn to page **22**.

➤ To become a test pilot, turn to page **26**.

We Can Do It!

"Rosie the Riveter" came to symbolize the many women who worked during the war.

You hate to hold in your anger about a man earning more money than you. But you need the steady income. And helping the war effort makes you feel good about yourself.

Turn the page.

When summer rolls around, you have a problem. Elizabeth is home from school and you have no one to watch her.

You place an ad for a babysitter in the local grocery store. Several teenage girls stop by your home to be interviewed. But none of them seem right.

Now what? You must ensure Elizabeth's safety, but you can't quit your job. You're thinking about taking in a trustworthy boarder who can live in your house and pay rent. You also have a chance to take the "graveyard shift" at work. That would allow you to work nights while your daughter is sleeping and be with her during the day.

➜ *To bring in a boarder, turn to page* **24**.

➜ *To take the graveyard shift, turn to page* **28**.

Turn the page.

You are tempted to travel to Texas for training as a test pilot. But you can't leave Elizabeth. Her father is already gone and may not come back. She can't lose her mother too.

But you know you must do something to contribute to the war effort. You hear that volunteers are needed at a canteen. When you stop by, the woman in charge explains what it's all about.

"This is where soldiers on leave from the war and others who are heading overseas come for entertainment, food, and drinks," she says. "We serve doughnuts and coffee and we host a dance once a month. We can sure use your help."

"I'd like that," you say enthusiastically.

Soldiers and sailors enjoyed the entertainment at a San Diego canteen in 1942.

You are not so sure you like it after a few minutes during your first shift. You hear angry words being exchanged between a sailor and a woman. Should you get in the middle of the argument or should you let them work it out for themselves?

→ To try to ignore it, turn to page **40**.

→ To get involved, turn to page **45**.

You're speaking with possible boarders and a woman named Gloria has brought you to tears.

"We were destroyed by the Depression," she says. "We had no money. And just when my husband found a job, he was drafted into the Army. He was shot and died three months ago."

Gloria begs you to allow her to stay with you even though she can't pay rent. She promises to take care of Elizabeth and do the cooking and cleaning. You can't say no.

Elizabeth couldn't be happier. She smiles as she talks about all the games she and Gloria play. She adds that Gloria has a nice boyfriend who stops by and that the two spend a lot of time in the basement.

You wonder why Gloria would have a boyfriend just a few months after her husband was killed. You become suspicious. You search the basement and find a large bundle hidden behind your sewing machine. It's wrapped in cloth that matches one of Gloria's dresses. You open the bundle. And to your shock, it's full of money!

You are tempted to use the money to pay bills, but you fear big trouble if you do. Maybe you should go to the police.

➻ To go to the police, turn to page **32**.

➻ To take the money, turn to page **44**.

It's August 1943. You hear from a college friend that the newly formed Women Airforce Service Pilots (WASP) is looking for female aviators for training. You have a pilot's license and flight experience. Perfect!

You leave Elizabeth in your mother's care and are accepted as a trainee in Sweetwater, Texas. When you arrive you speak to Jackie Cochran, the director of the WASP program. You admire Cochran, one of the greatest pilots in American history. She even set a national air speed record, flying from New York to Miami in just over four hours.

Cochran has words of warning for you. "This could be dangerous," she says. "You will be testing warplanes. They might not all be safe. But we must find out. Your mission is important for the safety of our bombers overseas."

Your first two missions go well. But on your third mission, the unthinkable happens.

Jackie Cochran (right) was a top racing pilot.

You're flying a twin-engine plane when you notice you are running out of fuel. The fuel gauge must be broken! You are flying over an area with many houses. You can try to bring the plane down, but you could land on a home and kill its residents. Or you can keep flying and hope to find an open area.

➤ To keep flying, turn to page 37.

➤ To bring the plane down, turn to page 42.

You never have liked the dark. But you have to overcome your fear and take the graveyard shift at the airplane factory. You need the job and your country needs workers.

It is often pitch black outside when you walk to work at midnight. No lights are allowed during air raid drills along the Atlantic coast. People are worried about a possible German attack on New York. Any lights that can be seen from warplanes would make a tempting target.

One night before you leave home you hear the sirens roaring. It's an air raid drill! Elizabeth is scared. You don't know if you should stay home with her and risk losing your job or go to work.

➻ To stay home, turn to page **34**.

➻ To go to work, turn to page **38**.

You have never been one to keep quiet when someone is taking advantage of you.

"Hey, Mr. Foster!" you greet your boss angrily. "Why am I making less money than the man I'm working with? I've been working here longer than he has and I do just as good a job."

"That's easy," he says. "You can't be doing as good a job. You're a woman. Women are weaker. This is hard, physical work."

"That's not true!" you yell. "I'm doing the same job just as well as any man here, and I should be paid the same!"

"How would you like to get paid nothing for having no job?" he asks.

Turn the page.

Men and women worked together to build planes for the war effort.

He's threatening to fire you. "I'd rather get paid nothing than work here," you tell Mr. Foster. "Either I get equal pay for equal work or I quit!"

"You won't have to quit," he answers. "You're fired!"

You storm out of the factory and walk home. You need money and now you have no job. You want to help the war effort and now you can't.

But you know that with so many men overseas there is a need for female workers. You start to feel better when you realize that other jobs are waiting for you. And you hope you'll be paid fairly.

THE END

To follow another path, turn to page 11.
To read the conclusion, turn to page 103.

You run to the police station and show an officer the cash.

"This money isn't stolen," says the officer. You are relieved, but only briefly. "It's counterfeit!" he says. "Phony money. Your boarder is a crook!"

You try to keep calm. The woman living in your house and her boyfriend are criminals. There was no dead husband. You're sure of it! She must have made up the entire story. And she's been spending every day with your daughter.

Soon the police raid your home. They arrest Gloria and her boyfriend.

The babysitter didn't work out. The boarder certainly didn't work out. You need the money, but keeping Elizabeth safe is more important. So you quit your job at the airplane factory and take another one as a waitress in a coffee shop. The owner lets Elizabeth stay with you until she returns to school.

A World War II poster called female workers "soldiers without guns."

You are not earning as much money, but it's worth it. For the first time in a long time, you have peace of mind.

THE END

To follow another path, turn to page 11.
To read the conclusion, turn to page 103.

The air raid siren is wailing. Elizabeth is shaking, and you are hugging her.

"I know it's a little frightening," you whisper in her ear. "You'll be fine. I have to go to work now."

"No, no, no!" Elizabeth screams as she bursts into tears. "Don't go, mommy!"

You think for a moment. You've never missed work. You figure one night won't hurt. You call your boss. You don't want to lie and tell him you're sick, so you tell him the truth.

"Every child in this city is scared right now," he bellows. "You get yourself into work or don't bother coming in again!"

You have no choice. You know what is more important—and it's not your job. After you calmly tell your boss you won't be in tonight, he slams down the phone.

Turn the page.

You'll stay home but you know you must have a serious talk with Elizabeth. You put your arm around her and speak softly.

"During the Depression, people were out of work," you tell her. "People were poor. Some people were homeless. But President Roosevelt told Americans something that made them feel strong. He said, 'The only thing we have to fear is fear itself.' That means you have nothing to be afraid of but being afraid. And that's what I want you to think about."

Elizabeth says nothing, but you can tell she's taking it to heart. You know she'll be fine.

But will you? You'll have to start looking for a new job tomorrow. But as you face your uncertain future, you know you made the right choice.

THE END

To follow another path, turn to page 11.
To read the conclusion, turn to page 103.

You sweat and tremble. You can't find anywhere to land your plane. You are over a crowded city. But you don't panic. You are thinking more clearly than you ever have before.

You hope you have enough fuel to get away from the heart of the city. You keep flying at a steady clip. Even a crash landing on water could save your life. As soon as you find even the smallest open spot, you will try to land safely.

Suddenly, all your hopes are dashed. The plane begins diving to the earth. You know you're going to die. You think about how odd it is that you will die in the war without leaving the United States. Tears well up in your eyes as you realize you'll never see Edward or Elizabeth again. Then everything goes black.

THE END

To follow another path, turn to page 11.
To read the conclusion, turn to page 103.

You comfort Elizabeth as best you can. You have agreed to take the graveyard shift and you are stuck with it.

You also have other worries. Shortages of food and household goods are making it hard to shop. Sometimes you must visit several stores to find what you need. Meat, sugar, paper products, and rubber goods are especially hard to find because they're needed in the war effort.

You receive ration stamps that can be used to buy certain items. You spend hours trying to figure out what to buy and what stamps to keep for later use.

You want to make Elizabeth a special cake for her birthday, but it calls for butter. You have ration stamps, but there's no butter to be found.

Items were in short supply during the war, and shoppers had to use ration books.

Poor Elizabeth. There will be no special cake this year. You know she'll understand. You've talked about the many children suffering in Europe. Going without cake is nothing compared with their ordeal.

Despite problems shopping, you feel you are in control of your life. But there is one thing that is out of your control. You have no idea if Edward will come home alive. All you can do is hope and pray.

THE END

To follow another path, turn to page 11.
To read the conclusion, turn to page 103.

You are trying to ignore the argument between the woman and the sailor. And you're doing fine—for a while. But suddenly you hear a loud slap. Now you have to get involved.

"He wouldn't leave me alone, so I had to slap him," the woman says.

"All I wanted was a little kiss," the sailor replies.

You are angry. You stand face-to-face with the sailor.

"You are a disgrace to that Navy uniform!" you tell him. "What do you have to say for yourself?"

You are surprised when he starts to cry.

"I'm just scared," he says through his tears. "I'm shipping out in two days. I'm afraid of getting killed."

You are no longer mad. You put your arm around the sailor.

"This is a frightening time for everyone," you say softly. "You shouldn't be ashamed of being scared. Our greatest American heroes were scared. But you can't go around bothering women. Do you understand?"

"Yes, I do," he replies. "Thank you for understanding, ma'am."

The sailor sits down quietly and appears to be in deep thought. You know you got through to him. In some small way, you feel as if you have helped the war effort. And that makes you proud.

41

THE END

To follow another path, turn to page 11.
To read the conclusion, turn to page 103.

You are desperate. Everywhere you look below there are houses. But you know that you could run out of fuel at any second.

Suddenly you notice a large open field. This could be your only chance to land your plane safely. It's a tricky landing. If you pull up too short, you will crash through the roof of a house. If you fly too far, you will put your plane onto a busy street.

You are coming in too fast! You fear for your life. You finally slow the plane, but you're headed for a big yellow house. You miss the house by about 100 feet and land the plane safely at the edge of the field.

Women Airforce Service Pilots were based and trained in Sweetwater, Texas.

You know as you stumble from the cockpit that your days as a test pilot are over. You can't take any more chances. The boys overseas are risking their lives, but you have a daughter to take care of here at home. You can't afford to be killed.

THE END

To follow another path, turn to page 11.
To read the conclusion, turn to page 103.

You grab a handful of money from the bundle and count it. It's more than $2,000!

You head for the bank to deposit the cash. No more money worries for you! But suddenly your mind starts racing. What if the money was stolen? What if Gloria is keeping the money safe for a relative? You might get arrested for theft! You sure couldn't take care of Elizabeth if you were in jail!

You stop right then and race back home. You put the money back into the cloth bundle. You know in your heart that you did the right thing. Greed nearly got the better of you. You vow that won't happen again.

THE END

To follow another path, turn to page 11.
To read the conclusion, turn to page 103.

You have the unruly sailor escorted from the canteen.

"Are you all right?" you ask the woman.

"I'm fine," she says. "But I'm never coming here again."

"Oh, please do!" you reply. "Most of the men here are very nice and respectful. I urge you to stay. They have either been fighting the war or they will be soon. They need a friendly face and a friendly voice."

She agrees. Within minutes she is talking quietly with a soldier. You are thrilled to see both of them smiling.

45

THE END

To follow another path, turn to page 11.
To read the conclusion, turn to page 103.

The Japanese attack on Pearl Harbor prompted hatred of Japanese-Americans.

CHAPTER 3

FIGHTING A WAR IN SAN DIEGO

You're sitting in the school lunchroom eating a peanut butter and jelly sandwich. Suddenly, your friend Tommy leans over and whispers in your ear.

"We're beating up Toki Yakumura after school," he says. "Pass the word."

"But he's a nice kid," you reply.

"We're beating him because he's a dirty Jap," Tommy says. "The Japanese attacked Pearl Harbor, and we're going to attack Toki with our fists."

Turn the page.

You don't understand. Toki is one of your best friends. He was born right here in San Diego. His parents own a grocery store. You always thought of the whole family as American. You often see their American flag flying in their front yard. And even if Toki is Japanese, what did he have to do with Pearl Harbor?

A Japanese-American shop owner erected a sign the day after Pearl Harbor.

The school bell rings. You see Toki walking quickly out of the classroom. Tommy is one of five boys walking right behind him. They begin chasing Toki. And you begin chasing them. Soon Toki is surrounded. He looks frightened.

"Why are you doing this?" you yell. "Don't touch Toki!"

"You're either going to help us beat up Toki or you're a traitor," Tommy says. "And we hate traitors."

You would never join the attack, but do you risk losing your friends to defend Toki? If you try to save him, the boys might beat you up as well.

→ *To run away, turn to page* **50**.

→ *To defend Toki, turn to page* **56**.

You're scared. Your friends begin to punch Toki, who can't defend himself against five boys. But you can't fight that many classmates either.

"Help me!" Toki yells to you.

"No!" you scream back. And you run away.

You feel horrible as you race home. You are angry with yourself for not helping Toki. You tell your father about the fight.

"Do you know what's going on in Germany and the rest of Europe right now?" he asks.

You wonder why he's talking about Europe. Toki is Japanese.

"In Europe the Nazis are doing the same things to Jews like us that your friends did to Toki today. They are beating them up. They are even killing them. Nobody should allow what happened to Toki. But as a Jewish boy, you should understand that even more."

You know your father is right. You vow to be nice to Toki, but you feel too ashamed to apologize. Weeks go by. In late February 1942, you visit Toki at his house. He answers the door and the words pour out of you.

"I'm sorry I didn't help you that day," you tell him. "You were always my friend, Toki. And I want you to keep being my friend."

Jewish families faced near certain death after they surrendered to Nazi soldiers.

Turn the page.

Toki accepts your apology but he has sad news. "We're moving away," he says.

"Oh no!" you say. "I hope it's not because everyone has been so mean to you."

"That's not it," he answers. "We don't want to move. The government is making us move. They're moving all Japanese-Americans in the western United States to internment camps. I guess everyone is afraid of us."

"Don't worry, Toki," you blurt out without thinking. "I'll hide you. Meet me behind my house at 8 o'clock tonight. I won't let them take you away."

➻ To hide Toki, go to page **53**.

➻ To think over your options, turn to page **63**.

That night you look to your left, then to your right. You make sure your parents can't see you out the window of your house.

"Quick, follow me!" you whisper to Toki.

He is right behind you. You open the door to the shed next to the garage. He follows you inside.

"You'll be safe here," you tell him. "Nobody is taking my friend to some stupid camp. I'm going to sneak food and a blanket out to you."

You walk back into your house and open the refrigerator. You grab an apple for Toki and start out the door. But you hear a familiar voice.

"Where are you going?" It's your father.

"I'm going to eat this apple out back," you reply nervously.

Turn the page.

Just then you hear a knock on the front door. You follow your father as he walks over to answer it. Much to your shock, you see that it's Toki's parents. They are in a panic.

"Do you know where Toki is?" his mother asks you.

You thought you could lie, but one look at Toki's mother changes your mind. She is so upset that she's shaking. "I'm hiding Toki in the shed out back," you tell her. "And I want to hide you and Mr. Yakimura too."

"That's so kind," says Toki's mother. "Your heart is in the right place. But we would all get into much trouble if you did that."

Soon Toki and his family are out of your house. Three days later they're out of your neighborhood. But before they leave, you talk one more time with Toki.

"Will you see us off at the train station?" he asks. "It would mean a lot to me."

"Sure!" you answer. "It's the least I can do for my best friend."

You weren't just being nice. You feel now that Toki is your best friend. But when you tell your father about Toki's invitation, he suggests you stay home where it's safe.

"There could be trouble at the station," he says. "Some people might show up to yell bad things to the Japanese families leaving for internment camps. I don't want you to experience that kind of hatred."

→ *To meet Toki at the train station, turn to page 58.*
→ *To stay away from the train station, turn to page 60.*

"Don't let them do this!" Toki yells out to you. He is being hit by five of your classmates. He is not hitting back. He is just covering up his face.

"Lousy Jap!" says one boy as he slugs Toki in the stomach.

You rush in and grab Toki by the arm. You push Tommy back and run away with Toki. You're both faster than the others. They chase you but give up.

"You're a traitor!" Tommy screams at you. "You're no friend of mine!"

That evening you tell your father what happened. You both visit the parents of the boys who beat up Toki. Most of them promise they will punish their kids for the attack, but not Tommy's father.

"I was the one who told Tommy to teach that kid a lesson," he says. "The Jap families here are going to help the people in Japan attack San Diego. You watch and see."

When you return home you receive a phone call from Charlie, one of your classmates who had been hitting Toki that afternoon.

"There is only one way we can stay friends now after you saved that kid," he says. "You have to prove your loyalty to the United States by destroying something Japanese. Be in the woods after school tomorrow."

The only Japanese things you can think of are your Mom's good dishes. You want your friends back, but you don't want to destroy her Noritake china.

→ To prove your loyalty in another way, turn to page 66.

→ To join your friends in the woods, turn to page 70.

A small crowd has gathered at the station. You see hundreds of Japanese-Americans hauling anything they can carry on wheels or on their backs. Among them are the Yakimuras.

You have time to say a quick good-bye before you hear something that makes you mad.

"Good riddance, Japs!" screams a man in the crowd. "Don't come back!" shouts another. "This is for Pearl Harbor!" bellows an old woman.

You can't help yourself. "Hey! Shut up!" you yell. "Those are my friends!"

Suddenly you are surrounded. Every face looks angry. "Your friends, huh?" says a young man. "Maybe you should go with them! We're going to give you 10 seconds to get out of here."

Japanese-Americans were moved by train to internment camps in California and other states.

You have no choice. Everyone is bigger, stronger, and older than you are. You walk away, but you feel good about yourself. You stuck up for Toki and his family and you showed some courage.

THE END

To follow another path, turn to page 11.
To read the conclusion, turn to page 103.

Toki is not in school, of course. You thought you were the only kid who knew why. "Toki and his family are leaving for the internment camp," you tell your classmates. "It makes me sad."

"I'm sure not sad," Tommy says. "My father is planning a special surprise party for them."

"What do you mean?" you ask Tommy angrily. "What are you planning?"

"Let's just say the Yakimuras will know how we feel about the Japs when they're getting on that train," Tommy says. "My dad and I even bought some eggs and tomatoes to throw at them."

You wish you could be at the station. But your dad really didn't want you to go. You have to wait until school the next day to find out what happened. You decide that if Tommy had a surprise for Toki, you would have a surprise for Tommy.

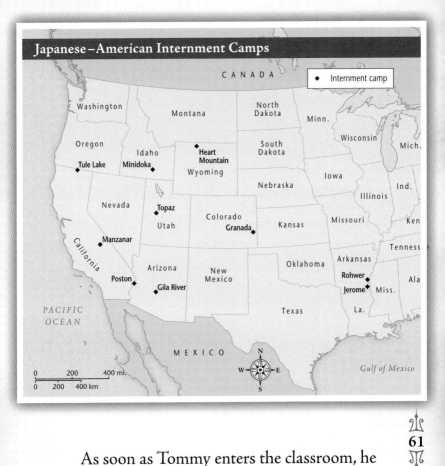

Japanese–American Internment Camps

◆ Internment camp

CANADA

Washington

Montana

North Dakota

Minn.

Oregon

Idaho

Wisconsin

Mich.

Tule Lake ◆

◆ Heart Mountain

South Dakota

Minidoka ◆

Wyoming

Iowa

Ind.

Nebraska

Illinois

Nevada

◆ Topaz

Utah

Colorado

Granada ◆

Kansas

Missouri

Ken

California

◆ Manzanar

Arizona

New Mexico

Oklahoma

Arkansas

Tenness

◆ Poston

◆ Gila River

Rohwer ◆

Ala

PACIFIC OCEAN

Jerome ◆ Miss.

Texas

La.

MEXICO

Gulf of Mexico

0   200   400 mi.
0 200 400 km

N
W E
S

As soon as Tommy enters the classroom, he makes an announcement to the class. "I hit Toki with a tomato just before he got on the train!" he says with a laugh.

Turn the page.

But you're ready to get revenge for Toki. You brought a tomato to school. At recess you pull it out and rub it in Tommy's face.

"That's for Toki!" you yell.

Tommy jumps on you and you start fighting in the mud. Your teacher, Mrs. Stone, pulls you apart.

"What happened to you two?" she asks. "You used to be best friends."

"Not anymore," you reply. "And not ever again."

You have mud and tomato all over you. But you've never felt so proud. Toki will never know it, but you defended his honor.

THE END

To follow another path, turn to page 11.
To read the conclusion, turn to page 103.

You've been having doubts about your plan to hide Toki. But you are surprised when he comes to the front door of your house.

"Why aren't you hiding?" you ask.

"I have to be with my family," says Toki. "We always stick together." As he slowly turns to leave, you realize your plan wouldn't have worked. But you feel so sad.

You are sitting in your bedroom with your head in your hands. Your father comes in. "What's wrong?" he asks. You explain your plan to him.

He agrees that your plan wouldn't work. "But I'm proud of you," he says. "It showed that you have feelings for other people."

"But Dad," you reply, "if we as a Jewish family were in Germany right now, wouldn't you want someone to hide us?"

Turn the page.

Posted notices warned Japanese-Americans of their pending evacuation.

Your father is deep in thought. "This isn't Germany," he finally says. "I know in my heart that our government will treat the Japanese-Americans much better than the Jews are being treated in Germany."

You still feel terrible for Toki and his family.

"In times of war," says your father, "people get carried away by fear. That makes them do things that are wrong. I want you to think about that."

You do think about it. You hate the Japanese who bombed Pearl Harbor, but you don't think Toki or any innocent person should be punished for it. You're afraid it will take Americans a long time to face up to that truth.

THE END

To follow another path, turn to page 11.
To read the conclusion, turn to page 103.

Your classmates want to know if you're going to destroy something from Japan. And suddenly a thought pops into your mind.

"No, I have a better plan to prove my loyalty," you say.

You remember hearing that your Scout troop was going to have a scrap metal drive. Your metal cars, trucks, trains, and other toys could be melted down to make weapons and equipment for the war.

At the next Boy Scout meeting, you ask your scout leader about the scrap metal drive. Mr. Landon explains that it's starting next week. He also says the Scouts will be searching for old tires and other rubber goods that can be turned into tank treads and tires for jeeps. You will also be looking for newspapers and other kinds of paper. It can be recycled to make material for packages sent overseas.

Bicycle tires and other rubber items were recycled.

As months go by, you read the paper and listen to the radio for news about the war. The more you learn, the more you want to help. One day your mom puts a thought into your mind.

Turn the page.

BUY WAR BONDS

"I'll tell you what," she says. "We'll pay you to do chores around the house. Once you get enough money, you can fill up your Victory Book."

You received your Victory Book weeks ago. You need to fill it up with stamps, which cost a dime each. Once you've placed 187 stamps in it, plus pay 5 cents, you can buy a war bond worth $18.75. The money goes to the war effort. In 10 years you can cash in the war bond for $25.

You've come a long way since the war began. You realize that Toki and his parents are good Americans even if they are of Japanese ancestry. And you know now that putting your toys and time to good use is far more helpful than destroying something made in Japan.

THE END

To follow another path, turn to page 11.
To read the conclusion, turn to page 103.

You're lucky your parents aren't home. You run to the dining room and gather plates, cups, and saucers and place them in a box. Soon you're racing through the woods. You find your friends in a small clearing.

"So you decided to show up," says Tommy. "Maybe you can prove your loyalty and we can still be friends."

"Of course," you reply. "I want to still be friends. I hate the Japanese we're fighting in the war. But I like Toki. What did Toki have to do with the bombing of Pearl Harbor?"

Your friends don't have an answer for you.

You dump the Japanese-made dishes on the ground. Tommy says that each of you will take turns smashing the dishes into little pieces. He says that you can go first.

You begin smashing away at the china. But it doesn't make you feel good or loyal. And now you are really mad at your friends.

"This is stupid!" you yell at Tommy. "My mom is going to have a fit! And how does this help us win the war?"

"Just go home, you traitor!" he screams.

"I'll go home," you reply. "But we're not friends anymore."

As you walk home to tell your mother what happened, you realize you don't even want to be friends with Tommy. You realize Toki is a much better friend.

71

THE END

To follow another path, turn to page 11.
To read the conclusion, turn to page 103.

TWICE A PATRIOT

EX-PRIVATE OBIE BARTLETT LOST LEFT ARM—PEARL HARBOR
RELEASED: DEC., 1941—NOW AT WORK WELDING
IN A WEST COAST SHIPYARD...

A patriotic war poster told the story of an Army private who lost his arm.

"Sometimes I feel my job here is as important as the one I had to leave."

CHAPTER 4

FIGHTING TWO WARS

You would like to shake hands with your 22-year-old son Albert, but you can't. You have no right arm.

It's March 1943. Albert is greeting you at the bus station in your hometown of Mobile, Alabama. You haven't seen him since you left to fight the war more than a year earlier. Your 24th Infantry Regiment was one of the first regiments to ship out. The American military is still segregated—blacks cannot fight alongside whites. So although trained in combat, you and other African-Americans were often placed in service roles instead.

Turn the page.

But bullets couldn't tell the difference between black and white, soldier and worker. Three weeks ago, on an island near Australia, a stray bullet shattered your arm. It had to be amputated. Now here you are, back home and out of the Army.

Although you are proud of your service overseas, you're looking forward to your new life. You saw enough of the horrors of war.

You hope the war has helped bring about changes in Alabama. Ever since birth you and others like you have been discriminated against in every walk of life.

You quickly find out nothing has changed. You risked your life for your country, but your country treats you as an inferior person. You know that African-Americans are mistreated in the North as well, but they can at least go to the same public places as whites.

African-Americans were often restricted to segregated theaters in the South.

You recall an invitation from your old friend Sam to live with him and his family on his Illinois farm.

You are sick of Alabama. You will never forget what happened five years ago when your wife became ill. She died because a nearby hospital served only white patients and refused to admit her. By the time she arrived at the hospital for blacks, she was dead. But still, you have friends and relatives here. Do you take your family and move?

➻ *To move to Illinois, turn to page* **76.**

➻ *To stay in Alabama, turn to page* **78.**

You send a telegram to your friend Sam stating that you are coming to live with him. You begin packing your truck.

"What are you doing?" your younger son, Jack, asks.

"We're moving to Illinois," you reply. "I will not live as a second-class citizen anymore. We're fighting for freedom in Europe and Asia, and we have no freedom here in Alabama. Go tell Albert we're leaving."

Albert races into the room.

"Good!" he says. "I'm glad we're going. I can't get out of Alabama fast enough."

You are soon on your way to Illinois. When you arrive, Sam and his wife, Mary, take you and your sons to a nearby restaurant. You eat in the same room as whites for the first time in your life. It gives you a good feeling.

That good feeling disappears quickly when 18-year-old Jack opens his mouth.

"Dad, I want to serve in the Army, just like you did," he says. "They need me over there."

You know that is true. The Germans control almost all of Europe, and the Japanese are fierce fighters.

You also know that Jack could be killed. Why should he die for a country that treats African-Americans so badly? But you are proud of his courage.

➤ To encourage Jack to volunteer, turn to page **80**.

➤ To try to stop Jack from volunteering, turn to page **85**.

You enjoy getting a haircut because it allows you to sit quietly and think. So the week after you return home, you stop by the barbershop.

As you watch bits of your hair falling to the floor, you ponder whether to leave Alabama or join your friend on his farm in Illinois. You ask your barber, Joe, for his opinion.

"You have every good reason to leave," he says. "Our people are treated better up North than they are here. But I think you should stay. You owe something to the people of Mobile to help change things. Wouldn't it be great if someday Negroes could vote or go to the park with whites or attend the same schools? Maybe you can help make that happen."

You agree. By the time he is done clipping your hair, you have decided to stay.

A few weeks later, a letter from the draft board arrives. It's addressed to Albert. You know what it is before he opens it. Albert has been drafted.

An angry look appears on Albert's face as he reads the letter. He slams it on the table.

"I'm not fighting in any war for the United States," he says. "I went to an inferior school because I'm black. I can't vote because I'm black. In the eyes of Alabama, I'm not even good enough to swim in the same pool or sit in the same restaurant as a white person. Why should I help a country that won't help me?'"

"You have no choice," you say. "You've been drafted. You have to go."

"We'll see about that," he says.

➤ To let Albert make his own decision, turn to page **96**.

➤ To convince him to report, turn to page **97**.

You look Jack straight in the eye and point to your right shoulder.

"Do you see this shoulder?" you ask him. "It means good luck to me."

"Good luck?" Jack answers with a puzzled look on his face. "How can it be good luck? There is no arm attached to that shoulder."

"There could have been no body attached to it," you respond. "I could have been killed. I was very lucky. But you might not be so lucky if you go off to fight. Is it worth risking your life for a country that thinks we are inferior to whites?"

"Yes, it is," Jack says. "I heard stories that the Germans are killing Jewish people all over Europe. They are murdering people in the countries they take over. We must defeat them."

"That's all I wanted to hear," you say. "I'm proud of you for standing up for what is right. Maybe if we risk our lives and do what's right overseas, then someday soon the leaders of this nation will do what's right for us right here in the United States."

Two days later Jack is gone. A few weeks later you receive a letter from him. He's training with the mostly African-American 92nd Infantry Division. You know he'll see combat in Europe.

Now it's Albert who has a question. He doesn't like farm life. He learned that factories making jeeps for the war are seeking workers in Detroit, Michigan. He wants to move there. You worry he could get into trouble living in Detroit on his own.

→ To move with Albert to Detroit, turn to page **82**.

→ To stay on the farm, turn to page **91**.

Sam is in the barn milking a cow.

"Sam, it was so nice of you to invite my family to live with you. But Albert and I are moving to Detroit. They need factory workers there. I'm sorry to leave."

A few days later you're driving to Detroit. It's early June 1943 and you are feeling good. But after one week on his factory job, Albert tells you something that turns your mood from joy to anger.

"I was talking with one of the white guys at the factory who started on the job last week," he says. "He told me he's going to get promoted long before I do. And even worse, I'm going to be put in a more dangerous job than he is. When I asked him why, he told me it was because I was a Negro."

You're mad, but not shocked. You know that African-Americans aren't just mistreated in the South. It happens nearly everywhere.

Blacks and whites worked together in wartime factories.

You realized that several days earlier when you were looking for an apartment. Some signs in front of the buildings read "No Negroes Allowed." You finally find an apartment that houses blacks in a section of town called Paradise Valley. It's not nearly as nice as the ones in which white people are living.

Turn the page.

Albert is upset about the discrimination you are dealing with. He hopes joining his new friends for some fun at the Belle Isle amusement park will take his mind off his troubles.

You're at home that night listening to music on the radio. Suddenly a news report interrupts the broadcast. Fighting has broken out between black teenagers and white sailors and teens. It began at the amusement park and spilled out into the city. You are worried.

➻ To look for Albert, turn to page **88**.

➻ To wait for him, turn to page **94**.

A restaurant is no place to talk to Jack about making the biggest decision of his young life. You wait until you get to your new home on your friend's farm. Then you speak to Jack at the kitchen table. "Why did we leave Alabama?" you ask. You already know the answer.

"Because of segregation," he answers. "A Negro can't reach his potential in Alabama."

"Has the United States government done anything to help Negroes in the South?" you ask.

Jack ponders the question. "I guess not," he says.

"When I got back home, I thought I would be treated with respect. But I was wrong. Our leaders have done nothing for us in the South. And we're treated badly in other parts of the country too. I don't want you helping this country until it shows it can help us."

Turn the page.

Your words make sense to you, but not to Jack. He has not changed his mind.

"I still want to join the Army just like you did," he says.

Jack says nothing for two days. You start hoping that you have convinced him to stay on the farm. But one morning he is not at the breakfast table. You knock on his door to wake him up, but there is no answer. You peek inside. The bed is made and he is gone. There's a note on a nearby chair. It reads:

Dear Dad and Albert:

By the time you read this, I will be on a bus to New York. I am off to join the war. I will make you both proud.

Love, Jack

African-American soldiers stand at attention during an army inspection.

You are angry that Jack went against your wishes. But you can't help but be proud of him too. You just hope and pray he will return home alive.

THE END

To follow another path, turn to page 11.
To read the conclusion, turn to page 103.

Visions of Albert being hurt race through your mind. You can't sit and do nothing. Soon you're driving downtown. You see police cars everywhere. You can't drive through, so you park and approach one of the police officers.

"Just go home!" the officer says. "Can't you see that we have a riot on our hands here?"

You are about to leave when you notice Albert. He looks confused and scared. He has blood all over his face and hands.

"That's my son, that's my son!" you tell the officer. "I must get him out of here! Albert! Albert!"

He sees you and runs as fast as he can to you. You grab his bloody hand and race toward the car. You hear gunshots and pray one doesn't find you or your son. You finally feel safe when you reach the car and start driving home.

Police fired tear gas as white rioters fled a black neighborhood in Detroit.

Soon Albert is telling you all about the riot. "When we got to the amusement park," he says, "some white teenagers and sailors were beating up some of our friends. We had to defend our buddies, so we joined the fight. Before you knew it, more guys got involved and there was a big battle."

Turn the page.

"Pretty soon it was a riot," he continues. "The fighting spilled over into the city. Negroes were attacking any white people they saw. And whites were attacking innocent Negroes. It was horrible."

"What were you doing?" you ask.

"By that time I was just watching. I wanted to get out of there. But the police couldn't control what was going on. Three white guys attacked me. That's how I got all bloody. Then the police starting shooting. I lay there so I wouldn't get hit by bullets. When the shooting was over, there were a bunch of people dead on the ground. But stop worrying. I'm all right now."

"You're going to stay all right," you reply. "We're leaving Detroit and going back to Sam's farm. At least there we can find some peace."

THE END

To follow another path, turn to page 11.
To read the conclusion, turn to page 103.

You remember listening to President Roosevelt on the radio. He often said that every American must do his or her part to win the war.

You tried to do your part in the Army. But even though you lost your right arm, you feel there is more you can do. You decide to stay on Sam's farm and help grow food for the war effort.

Albert is big and strong and finds the farm work difficult but satisfying. He has even talked about owning his own farm someday. You'd like to help more, but you can't do heavy labor. So you decide you can help Sam make the most out of his farm.

You head to Alabama to talk to a farmer named Buck you met years ago. Buck had learned farming techniques in the early 1930s from a Tuskegee Institute graduate. The man trained years earlier under the great African-American scientist George Washington Carver.

Turn the page.

We CAN'T win this war without sacrifice on the home front, too.

You spend two weeks learning everything you can about farming from Buck. He shows you the best way to treat the soil, rotate and water the crops, and the best crops to grow in various climates.

You return to Illinois and show Sam everything Buck taught you. Sam is impressed. He sits at his kitchen table and studies the information. With you and Albert helping, he treats the soil in his fields just as Buck explained.

"Look at my crops," Sam says several months later. "They are growing bigger and better than they ever have. And I have you and Buck to thank for it. The soldiers who eat these vegetables won't go away hungry. Maybe your son Jack will end up eating one of these carrots!"

You feel as if you have indeed done your job to help the war effort. You can't do too much work on the farm with one arm. But as President Roosevelt said, you do what you can. And you feel proud.

THE END

To follow another path, turn to page 11.
To read the conclusion, turn to page 103.

You are frozen with fear. You think about driving downtown to try to find Albert. But you don't think you can track him down.

Suddenly the phone rings. The noise and your fear combine to make you jump from your chair. You answer the phone. It's the police.

"We are sorry, but we have reason to believe that your son was killed in the riot tonight," says the voice on the other end. "We need you to come down to the morgue and identify the body."

You feel as if all the life has drained out of you. You can barely drag yourself to your car. You don't know if you can concentrate on driving two miles to the morgue. But even though you are in a daze, you make it safely. An attendant meets you at the door and takes you to a back room. A body with a sheet over it awaits you. The sheet is pulled back.

"Is this your son?" you are asked.

It is Albert. There is a bullet hole in his neck. You say nothing. You just nod and walk away. You have never felt such grief.

Only one thought is going through your mind. You wish you had gone downtown to find Albert and get him away from the violence. If you had, perhaps he would still be alive. Maybe you would have been killed. But you would have gladly given your life to save Albert.

And now it is too late.

THE END

To follow another path, turn to page 11.
To read the conclusion, turn to page 103.

Albert's bags are packed. And soon he's gone. He told you he was reporting for the draft, and you hope it's true.

A week later you receive a letter in the mail. There is no return address. A feeling of shock and horror washes over you as you read it.

"I have sneaked out of training," Albert writes. "I will tell nobody where I am. I will not fight for this country. I am headed to Canada, where I can be treated more like a man than I can here."

Your mind is racing. You know if Albert gets caught, he's going to jail. And you know wherever he goes, he'll have to deal with hatred from some people.

Will you ever see him again? Tears start rolling down your cheeks. You can only hope that someday, you'll be reunited.

THE END

To follow another path, turn to page 11.
To read the conclusion, turn to page 103.

African-Americans were allowed to enlist in the Army Air Corps for the first time in 1941.

You walk slowly to the door and stand in front of it. You hold up the only arm you have.

"I will not let you leave this house," you tell Albert sternly. "You are going to report to basic training and you will fight overseas. Your country needs you."

"How do they need me?" Albert asks.

Turn the page.

"The Germans are not just treating Jews and others badly like Negroes are being treated here," you say. "They are killing millions of people. They are trying to take over the world. They must be stopped. You would be fighting to save the world."

You have made an impression on your son. You leave him alone to think. Five minutes later, he visits you in the kitchen.

"You're right," he says. "I never thought about it that way. I will report."

You are proud when Albert volunteers to be trained as a Tuskegee Airman. You are even more proud when he performs so well that he is sent overseas to fly a P-51 Mustang fighter plane.

He writes how he and his fellow pilots painted the tails on their planes bright red. That way the American bombers they were escorting, as well as the German pilots, would know who they were.

Pilots posed on an airplane at the Tuskegee Army Airfield during World War II.

Many months pass. On a cold morning in February 1945, you notice two soldiers walking toward your house. One is carrying a telegram. Before they even reach your door, you know the bad news they're bringing. Albert has been killed in action.

Turn the page.

"Your son has died a hero," says one soldier. "He was shot down on a mission over Germany. Your son was a fine pilot. You should be proud."

You are proud. But as you sit on the couch and cry, you wonder if you did the right thing by talking Albert into fighting the war.

You know that Albert wasn't alone. Thousands of American troops have been killed. You realize that Albert was doing his duty. As he said, he was trying to help save the world.

You know that you will shed more tears as time goes by. But you also know that the soldier was right: Albert indeed died a hero.

100

THE END

To follow another path, turn to page 11.
To read the conclusion, turn to page 103.

The Tuskegee Airmen flew more than 15,000 missions in Africa, Italy, and Germany.

About 3 million women worked in military factories during the war.

CHAPTER 5

A NEW WORLD

World War II changed life for everyone—those who fought and those who stayed on the home front.

Most women returned to their lives as housewives after the war. But those who helped the war effort by taking jobs felt a sense of pride and satisfaction. Their efforts planted the seeds of the women's movement a generation later. By the early 1970s, women were forging careers all over the United States.

A Japanese-American child awaited evacuation in California.

After the war Japanese Americans slowly rebuilt their lives. In 1976, the 200th anniversary of the founding of the country, the president of the United States admitted mistakes were made on the home front during World War II.

President Gerald Ford said, "We now know what we should have known then—not only was that evacuation wrong, but Japanese-Americans were and are loyal Americans."

The contributions made by black soldiers in World War II forever changed their position in the United States. Soon after the war, the armed services integrated. No longer were blacks separated from whites. They would fight side-by-side in future wars. Soon blacks began demanding and winning equality in all walks of American life.

Americans gained confidence through their efforts as soldiers and on the home front during World War II. They felt great pride at helping return peace and freedom to the people of Europe and Asia. And as President Roosevelt asked, everyone seemed to do his or her part.

TIMELINE

1939—World War II begins as Germany invades Poland September 1.

France and Great Britain declare war on Germany two days later.

1940—President Franklin D. Roosevelt asks Congress for more money for military spending in May.

France surrenders to Germany in June.

Congress enacts the first peacetime draft in American history

1941—The Lend-Lease program, in which the United States provides war material for countries fighting Germany, is signed into law.

Tuskegee Institute in Tuskegee, Alabama, begins training black pilots.

Japanese warplanes bomb Pearl Harbor December 7; the U.S. declares war on Japan the next day.

Japan, Italy and Germany declare war on the United States.

1942—An order signed by President Roosevelt declares that all Americans of Japanese descent living in the western U.S. must be relocated.

Rationing of such items as coffee and gasoline begins.

1943—Race riots strike Detroit in June.

1944—One June 6 Allied forces land in France as the D-Day invasion begins.

France is liberated from German rule as Allied forces march into Paris in August.

German troops launch the Battle of the Bulge in Belgium in December.

1945—Franklin Roosevelt dies April 12 and is succeeded as president by Harry Truman.

German dictator Adolf Hitler commits suicide April 30; Germany surrenders May 7.

An atomic bomb is dropped on the Japanese city of Hiroshima August 6; another atomic bomb is dropped on the Japanese city of Nagasaki three days later.

Japan formally surrenders September 2, ending the war.

OTHER PATHS TO EXPLORE

In this book you've seen how the events experienced during World War II look different from three points of view.

Perspectives on history are as varied as the people who lived it. You can explore other paths on your own to learn more about what happened. Seeing history from many points of view is an important part of understanding it.

Here are ideas for other World War II points of view to explore:

+ Japanese-Americans weren't the only people not trusted during World War II. What would it have been like to be of German or Italian descent in the United States during wartime?

+ Some men who wanted to fight in the war were classified as "4-F." That meant they were physically unable to go into battle. What would it have been like not being able to serve?

+ The most noted canteens during World War II featured movie stars and other famous people entertaining American troops. What would it have been like to spend time at such places?

READ MORE

Adams, Simon. *World War II*. New York: DK Pub., 2004.

Price, Sean. *Rosie the Riveter: Women in World War II*. Chicago: Raintree/Fusion, 2009.

Wagner, Melissa, and Dan Bryant. *The Big Book of World War II*. Philadelphia: RP Classics, 2009.

Williams, Brenda. *The Home Front*. Chicago: Heinemann Library, 2006.

INTERNET SITES

FactHound offers a safe, fun way to find Internet sites related to this book. All of the sites on FactHound have been researched by our staff.

Here's all you do:
Visit *www.facthound.com*
Type in this code: 9781429660198

GLOSSARY

combat (KOM-bat)—fighting between people or armies

depression (di-PRE-shuhn)—a period during which business, jobs, and stock values decline or stay low

dictator (DIK-tay-tuhr)—someone who has complete control of a country, often ruling it unjustly

draft (DRAFT)—a system that chooses people who are compelled by law to serve in the military

infamy (IN-fuh-mee)—a lasting, widespread, and deep-rooted evil reputation brought about by something criminal, shocking, or brutal

isolationist (eye-so-LAY-shuhn-ist)—follower of a policy in which one country does not get involved with the political, social, or economic affairs of other countries

ration (RASH-uhn)—the amount of food or supplies allowed by a government

segregation (seg-ruh-GAY-shuhn)—the practice of keeping groups of people apart, especially based on race

BIBLIOGRAPHY

African Americans in World War II. Lest We Forget Network. 29 July 2011. www.lwfaam.net/ww2/

American Red Cross Canteens During World War II. American Red Cross. 29 July 2011. www.redcross.org/museum/history/WW2Canteens.asp

Binns, Stewart, and Adrian Wood. *America at War in Color.* Lincolnwood, Ill.: Contemporary Books, 2000.

Current Affairs 92nd Infantry Division. Indiana Military. 29 July 2011. www.indianamilitary.org/92nd/Current%20Affairs/CurrentAffairs.htm

Detroit Race Riots 1943. *The American Experience.* 29 July 2011. www.pbs.org/wgbh/amex/eleanor/peopleevents/pande10.html

Harris, Mark Jonathan, Franklin D. Mitchell, and Steven J. Schechter. *The Homefront: America During World War II.* New York: Putnam, 1984

Home Sweet Home Front: Dayton During World War II. Dayton History Books Online. 29 July 2011. www.daytonhistorybooks.com/page/page/1652502.htm

Legends of Tuskegee. National Park Service. 29 July 2011. www.nps.gov/museum/exhibits/tuskegee/

Pearl Harbor: Bulletin from Honolulu. Voices of World War II: Experiences From the Front and at Home. 29 July 2011. http://library.umkc.edu/spec-col/ww2/transcriptions/pearlharbor-bulletin.htm

Tuskegee Airmen History. Tuskegee Airman, Inc. 29 July 2011. www.tuskegeeairmen.org/Tuskegee_Airmen_History.html

INDEX